The Family Catechism

The Family Catechism

Fr. Francisco Radecki, CMRI

ISBN Number: 0-9715061-1-6

Library of Congress Control Number:

2004195212

Printed by Bookmasters, Inc., Mansfield, Ohio.

Design Editor: Amanda Diehl

Published by:

St. Joseph's Media

P.O. Box 186

Wayne, Michigan

48184-0186

Acknowledgments

Our Lord said, "Amen I say to you, unless you turn and become like little children, you will not enter into the kingdom of heaven." (Matthew 18: 3)   This book was written to lead little ones and their parents to Heaven.

This book was composed by the combined effort of many individuals, including three sets of twins. I would like to especially thank my twin, Fr. Dominic Radecki, CMRI and the Marian Priests;   Fr. Michael Anaya; the Marian Sisters; and the Burnor, Cichos, Diehl, Krizan, Lessnau, Sabella, Stratis, Taylor and Tibai families for their kind assistance.

Illustrations were drawn by Amanda Diehl, Barbara Hopkins, Mary Krizan; Natalie, Angela and Monica Sabella, Jessica Taylor, and Julie, Melissa, Melanie, Benjamin and Monica Tibai.

Sincere thanks to Paula Storm for her editorial assistance, Bob Valente for his technical support and a special thanks to Amanda Diehl for using her computer expertise to beautifully enhance the illustrations. May God bless them and the many others who have assisted in a variety of ways.

Dedicated to
the Holy Family,
the model of the
Catholic Family.

Catholic Prayers

The Sign of the Cross

In the Name of the Father, and of the Son, and of the Holy Ghost. Amen.

Morning Offering

O Jesus, through the Immaculate Heart of Mary, I offer Thee all my prayers, works, joys and sufferings of this day, for all the intentions of Thy Most Sacred Heart, in union with the Holy Sacrifice of the Mass throughout the world, in reparation for my sins, for the conversion of sinners, for the intentions of all our associates and for the relief of the Poor Souls in Purgatory.

I wish to gain all the indulgences attached to the prayers I shall say and to the good works I shall perform this day.

Our Father

(ENGLISH)	(LATIN)

Our Father, Who art in Heaven, hallowed be Thy Name; Thy Kingdom come; Thy will be done on earth as it is in Heaven. Give us this day our daily bread; and forgive us our trespasses as we forgive those who trespass against us; and lead us not into temptation, but deliver us from evil. Amen.

Pater noster, qui es in caelis: Sanctificetur nomen Tuum: Adveniat regnum tuum: Fiat voluntas Tua, sicut in caelo et in terra. Panem nostrum quotidianum da nobis hodie: Et dimitte nobis debita nostra, sicut et nos, dimittimus debitoribus nostris. Et ne nos inducas in tentationem. Sed libera nos a malo. Amen.

HAIL MARY

(ENGLISH)

Hail Mary, full of grace, the Lord is with thee. Blessed art thou among women and blessed is the fruit of thy womb, Jesus. Holy Mary, Mother of God, pray for us sinners, now and at the hour of our death. Amen.

(LATIN)

Ave, Maria, gratia plena; Dominus tecum: benedicta tu in mulieribus, et benedictus fructus ventris tui Jesus. Sancta Maria, Mater Dei, ora pro nobis peccatoribus, nunc et in hora mortis nostrae. Amen.

GLORY BE

(ENGLISH)	(LATIN)
Glory be to the Father, and to the Son and to the Holy Ghost. As it was in the beginning, is now and ever shall be, world without end. Amen.	Gloria Patri, et Filio, et Spiritui Sancto. Sicut erat in principio, et nunc et semper, et in saecula saeculorum. Amen.

APOSTLES CREED

I believe in God, the Father Almighty, Creator of Heaven and earth; and in Jesus Christ, His only Son, our Lord; Who was conceived by the Holy Ghost, born of the Virgin Mary, suffered under Pontius Pilate, was crucified, died and was buried. He descended into Hell; the third day He arose again from the dead; He ascended into Heaven, sitteth at the right hand of God, the Father Almighty; from thence He shall come to judge the living and the dead. I believe in the Holy Ghost, the Holy Catholic Church, the communion of saints, the forgiveness of sins, the resurrection of the body and life everlasting. Amen.

ANGELUS

(Prayed at noon and 6:00 p.m. during the year.)

(Versicle) The Angel of the Lord declared unto Mary.

(Response) And she conceived by the Holy Ghost.   Hail Mary...

(V.)   Behold the handmaid of the Lord.

(R.)   Be it done unto me according to thy word.   Hail Mary...

(V.)   And the Word was made flesh. (genuflect)

(R.)   And dwelt amongst us.   Hail Mary...

(V.)   Pray for us, O Holy Mother of God.

(R.)   That we may be made worthy of the promises of Christ.

Let us pray.

Pour forth we beseech Thee, O Lord, Thy grace into our hearts; that we, to whom the Incarnation of Christ Thy Son was made known by the message of an angel, may, by His Passion and Cross, be brought to the glory of His Resurrection. Through the same Christ our Lord. Amen.

HAIL HOLY QUEEN

Hail, holy Queen, Mother of mercy, our life, our sweetness and our hope! To thee do we cry, poor banished children of Eve! To thee do we send up our sighs, mourning and weeping in this valley of tears! Turn then, most gracious advocate, thine eyes of mercy towards us; and after this, our exile, show unto us the blessed fruit of thy womb, Jesus! O clement, O loving, O sweet Virgin Mary!

REGINA CAELI

(Prayed at noon and 6:00 p.m. during Easter time.)

(V.) Queen of Heaven, rejoice.   (R.) Alleluia.

(V.) For He Whom thou didst merit to bear.   (R.) Alleluia.

(V.) Hath risen as He said.   (R.) Alleluia.

(V.) Pray for us to God.   (R.) Alleluia.

(V.) Rejoice and be glad, O Virgin Mary, alleluia.

(R.) For the Lord has truly risen, alleluia.

Let us Pray

O God, Who by the Resurrection of Thy Son, Our Lord Jesus Christ, hast vouchsafed to make glad the whole world: grant, we beseech Thee, that through the intercession of the Virgin Mary, His Mother, we may attain the joys of eternal life. Through the same Christ our Lord. Amen.

MEMORARE

Remember, O most gracious Virgin Mary, that never was it known that anyone who fled to thy protection, implored thy help or sought thy intercession, was left unaided. Inspired with this confidence, I fly unto thee, O Virgin of virgins, my Mother! To thee do I come, before thee I stand, sinful and sorrowful. O Mother of the Word Incarnate, despise not my petitions, but in thy mercy hear and answer me. Amen.

GRACE BEFORE MEALS

Bless us, O Lord, and these Thy gifts, which we are about to receive from Thy bounty; through Christ Our Lord. Amen.

GRACE AFTER MEALS

We give Thee thanks, Almighty God, for all Thy benefits, Who livest and reignest forever and ever. May the souls of the faithful departed, through the mercy of God, rest in peace. Amen.

ACT OF FAITH

O my God, I firmly believe that Thou art one God in three Divine Persons, the Father, the Son and the Holy Ghost. I believe that Thy Divine Son became man and died for our sins, and that He will come to judge the living and the dead. I believe these and all the truths which the Holy Catholic Church teaches, because Thou hast revealed them, Who canst neither deceive nor be deceived.

ACT OF HOPE

O my God, relying on Thy almighty power and infinite mercy and promises, I hope to obtain the pardon of my sins, the help of Thy grace and life everlasting, through the merits of Jesus Christ, my Lord and Redeemer.

ACT OF CHARITY

O my God, I love Thee above all things, with my whole heart and soul, because Thou art all good and worthy of all my love. I love my neighbor as myself for the love of Thee. I forgive all who have injured me and I ask pardon of all whom I have injured.

PRAYER FOR THE FAITHFUL DEPARTED

Eternal rest grant unto them, O Lord and let perpetual light shine upon them. May they rest in peace. Amen.

PRAYER TO THE GUARDIAN ANGEL

Angel of God, my guardian dear,

To whom God's love commits me here;

Ever this day (night) be at my side,

To light and guard, to rule and guide. Amen.

The Blessed Trinity

God is a Spirit—the Supreme Being who made all things. God always was and always will be.

There are Three Persons in one God: the Father, the Son and the Holy Ghost. We call the Three Persons in one God the Blessed Trinity.

St. Patrick used a shamrock to simply explain the mystery of the Blessed Trinity. It has three leaves but is still only one shamrock.

Angels

Angels are pure spirits who do not have bodies. God loves everyone so much that He gives each person a special angel called a Guardian Angel. Everyone has a Guardian Angel to help them get to Heaven.

Your Guardian Angel prays for you, watches over you, protects you from danger and strengthens you to overcome temptation. Since your Guardian Angel is your best friend, you should pray to your special angel every day.

There are nine choirs (groups) of angels: Angels, Archangels, Thrones, Dominations, Principalities, Powers, Virtues, Cherubim and Seraphim. God tested the angels to see if they would love and obey Him. St. Michael and most of the angels remained faithful to God and are now in Heaven.

Devils

Sadly, many angels, led by Lucifer (Satan), disobeyed God and were cast into Hell where they will suffer forever. These bad angels, called devils, committed the first sin. When we are tempted we should always pray to God for help because the devils try to cause us to sin.

Saints

The holy men, women, boys and girls who once lived on earth and are now in Heaven are called saints. They are your friends and want you to be happy with them, too, after your life on earth is over. They pray for you and help you from Heaven. Saints lived very holy lives. You should read about them and try to be like them. If you are good, when you get to Heaven, you, too, will be a saint.

In your prayer book you will find many different kinds of saints:

- Confessors are holy men and boys.
- Popes and Bishops rule the Church.
- Doctors of the Church teach the Catholic Faith.
- Abbots are in charge of monasteries.
- Martyrs are men, women and children who died for Christ.
- Virgins dedicate their lives to Christ.
- Many Holy Women are also saints.

THE COMMUNION OF SAINTS IS MADE OF:

- The Church Triumphant   (Saints in Heaven)
- The Church Suffering   (Souls in Purgatory)
- The Church Militant   (Faithful Catholics on Earth)

Adam and Eve

God created Adam and Eve, the first man and woman. They lived happily in the Garden of Paradise. The greatest gift they received from God was sanctifying grace. This made them children of God and gave them the right to Heaven. God tested their love and obedience by commanding Adam and Eve not to eat the fruit of a certain tree. They had to choose between good (obeying God) and evil (disobeying God). Satan, disguised as a talking snake, told Eve that if she ate the fruit, she would become like God. Eve and Adam both ate the forbidden fruit. Because of their disobedience, Adam and Eve were punished by God and forced to leave Paradise.

Their worst punishment was the loss of sanctifying grace. As a result of their sin, the gates of Heaven were closed to Adam and Eve and also to all the members of the human race. The serious sin that Adam and Eve committed against Almighty God is called the original sin. We come into the world with original sin on our soul.

The Blessed Virgin Mary, because of her Immaculate Conception, was the only person ever created without original sin. Since Adam and Eve could not adequately make up for their terrible sin, God promised to send a Redeemer who would atone for their sin and open the gates of Heaven.

The Life of Jesus Christ

The Son of God came down from Heaven to earth in order to redeem us and open the gates of Heaven. Jesus Christ redeemed us by suffering and dying on the Cross for our sins. Jesus is both God and Man and was born in Bethlehem on Christmas morning. The Blessed Virgin Mary is called the Mother of God because Jesus Christ, her Son, is God. Jesus lived in Nazareth with His Blessed Mother and His foster father, St. Joseph. They are called the Holy Family.

By His words and example Jesus taught people how to be good and how to live holy lives. Jesus founded the Catholic Church and chose 12 men to be His Apostles. They helped Him with the important work of saving souls. Jesus performed many miracles in order to prove that He was God:

1) Jesus changed water into wine at the Marriage of Cana.
2) Jesus walked on the water of the Sea of Galilee.
3) Jesus fed thousands of people with just five loaves of bread and two fish.
4) Jesus calmed the stormy sea.
5) Jesus cured many sick people.
6) Jesus raised three people from the dead.
7) Jesus' greatest miracle took place on Easter Sunday when He rose from the dead by His own power.

On the first Good Friday, Jesus died on the Cross to make up for the sins of the world. Christ thereby proved His love for us and showed us how much sin hurts Him. Catholics do not eat meat on Fridays to remind themselves that Jesus died for the sins of the world on Good Friday.

In order to be forever happy with God in Heaven you must know, love and serve God on earth. The more you know about God and His goodness, the more you will love Him. You always want to spend time and talk with those you love. Every time you pray, you talk to God.

Grace is a special gift that God gives you every time you pray. Grace helps you to be good and keep the Ten Commandments. The Ten Commandments are the rules that everyone must obey in order to get to Heaven.

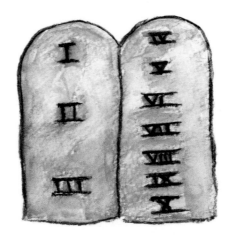

THE TEN COMMANDMENTS

1. I am the Lord thy God; thou shalt not have strange gods before Me.

2. Thou shalt not take the name of the Lord, thy God in vain.

3. Remember thou keep holy the Lord's day.

4. Honor thy father and thy mother.

5. Thou shalt not kill.

6. Thou shalt not commit adultery.

7. Thou shalt not steal.

8. Thou shalt not bear false witness against thy neighbor.

9. Thou shalt not covet thy neighbor's wife.

10. Thou shalt not covet thy neighbor's goods.

THE TEN COMMANDMENTS SIMPLIFIED FOR CHILDREN

1. I will love God and pray to Him every day.

2. I will always use God's name with love and respect.

3. I will go to Mass every Sunday and Holy Day.

4. I will obey my mom and dad.

5. I will be kind to everyone.

6. I will be pure in my words and actions.

7. I will respect the property of others.

8. I will always tell the truth.

9. I will be pure in my thoughts.

10. I will be content with what I have.

THE TEN COMMANDMENTS EXPLAINED

1. The first commandment teaches us that we must:

   - Love God above all things.

   - Pray to God every single day.

   - Love our Catholic Faith with all our hearts.

   - Always remain a Catholic.

1. The first commandment teaches us that we must not:

   - Love anything more than God.

   - Neglect to pray everyday.

   - Think about other things during our prayers.

   - Give up the practice of our Catholic Faith.

2. The second commandment teaches us that we must:

   - Respect God's name.

   - Always speak about God with reverence and love.

2. The second commandment teaches us that we must not:

   - Say God's name in anger.

   - Speak about God or the saints with disrespect.

   - Use phrases like "I swear to God."

3. The third commandment teaches us that we must:

   - Go to Mass on Sundays and Holy Days.

   - Dress properly for church.

   - Pay attention during Mass.

   - Treat Sundays as special days to love and honor God.

3. The third commandment teaches us that we must not:

- Miss Mass on purpose on Sundays and Holy Days.
- Laugh or talk in church.
- Distract others in church.
- Work or shop on Sundays or Holy Days.

4. The fourth commandment teaches us that we must:

- Obey our parents, teachers and those in authority.
- Love our parents and treat them with respect.

4. The fourth commandment teaches us that we must not:

- Disobey our parents, teachers and those in authority.
- Talk back to them or treat them with disrespect.
- Delay in obeying our parents.

5. The fifth commandment teaches us that we must:

- Be nice to everyone.
- Speak kindly of others.
- Use self control.

5. The fifth commandment teaches us that we must not:

- Talk badly of others.
- Become angry.
- Tease, argue or fight with others.

6. & 9. The sixth and ninth commandments teach us to:

- Be pure in thought, word and deed.
- Dress modestly.

6. & 9. The sixth and ninth commandments teach us not to:

- Watch impure TV, movies, DVD's or videos.

- Look at bad pictures, magazines, books or websites.

- Wear immodest clothes.

7. & 10. The seventh and tenth commandments teach us to:

- Be happy with what God and our parents give us.

7. & 10. The seventh and tenth commandments teach us not to:

- Take or damage things that belong to others.

- Want things that other people have.

8. The eighth commandment teaches us that we must:

- Always tell the truth.

- Always be honest.

8. The eighth commandment teaches us that we must not:

- Tell lies.

- Mislead others.

- Be jealous or greedy.

LAWS OF THE CHURCH

1. To assist at Mass on all Sundays and Holy Days of Obligation.

2. To fast and to abstain on the days appointed.

3. To confess our sins at least once a year.

4. To receive Holy Communion during the Easter time.

5. To contribute to the support of the Church.

6. To observe the Church's laws concerning marriage.

LAWS OF THE CHURCH SIMPLY EXPLAINED

1. Go to Mass on every Sunday and Holy Day.
2. Don't eat meat on Fridays and other abstinence days.
3. Go to confession at least once a year.
   (Try to go to confession once every 3 weeks.)
4. Go to Holy Communion once during Easter time.
   (Try to go to Holy Communion as often as you can.)
5. Do what you can to help your parish.
6. Catholics should marry Catholics.

HOLY DAYS OF OBLIGATION IN THE UNITED STATES

January 1	Circumcision of Our Lord
	(Jesus gets His name)
10 Days after Easter	Ascension Thursday
	(Jesus ascends into Heaven)
August 15	Assumption of Mary
	(Mary is taken up to Heaven)
November 1	All Saints' Day
	(A day we honor all the saints)
December 8	Immaculate Conception
	(Mary without sin)
December 25	Christmas
	(Jesus' birthday)

THE SEVEN SACRAMENTS

Jesus Christ lived on earth for 33 years and founded the Catholic Church. Our Lord taught us the way to Heaven and gave us the Seven Sacraments to bestow upon us the graces we need to be holy. A Sacrament is an outward sign, instituted by Christ to give grace.

BAPTISM

The sacrament that washes away original sin from your soul, the sin inherited from Adam and Eve, is called Baptism. It makes you an adopted child of God and gives you sanctifying grace—the grace that makes you holy. This grace is your ticket to Heaven. Sanctifying grace must be protected because it can be lost by mortal sin.

PENANCE

The sacrament that forgives the sins you commit after Baptism is called Penance.

Sin

Sin is a willful thought, word, deed (action) or omission forbidden by the law of God. There are two main kinds of sin: mortal and venial.

A mortal sin is a serious sin that hurts God very much. Purposely missing Mass on Sunday or stealing expensive things are mortal sins. God will not let anyone into Heaven who has an unforgiven mortal sin on his or her soul.

Three things that make a sin Mortal:

1) It's a big sin. (It is seriously wrong.)
2) You know it's a big sin.

   (You know it's seriously wrong.)
3) You do it anyway. (Full consent of the will.)

If you have committed a mortal sin, say the Act of Contrition right away and go to confession as soon as possible.

A venial sin is a lesser sin, but it still offends God. Disobeying, fighting and lying are venial sins.

All your sins can be forgiven by the priest in confession if you are really sorry for them. If you ever commit a mortal sin, do not be afraid to tell the priest. He takes Jesus' place and will never tell your sins to anyone.

How to Go to Confession

After you enter the confessional, kneel down, make the Sign of the Cross and say:

"Bless me, Father, for I have sinned. My last confession was_____(weeks or months ago)."

If this is your first confession, say, *"Bless me, Father, for I have sinned. This is my first confession."*

Tell the priest your sins and how many times you have committed them. When you have finished confessing your sins say,

"I am sorry for these and all the sins of my past life, especially (then mention a sin you are sorry for that you have already confessed)."

The priest will talk to you and give you a penance (some prayers) and will tell you to say the Act of Contrition.

Then say the Act of Contrition while the priest recites prayers in Latin (absolution) that forgives your sins. When the priest has finished, return to your place and say the prayers that were given to you for your penance.

THE ACT OF CONTRITION

O my God, I am **heartily sorry** for having **offended** Thee, and I **detest** all my sins, because I **dread** the loss of Heaven and the pains of Hell, but most of all because they offend Thee, my God, Who art all good and deserving of all my love. I **firmly resolve**, with the help of Thy grace, to confess my sins, to do penance and to **amend my life**. Amen.

EXPLANATION OF THE WORDS

heartily sorry (sorry from your heart)

offended (hurt)

detest (hate)

dread (fear)

firmly resolve (try real hard)

amend my life (try to never sin again)

EXAMINATION OF CONSCIENCE FOR CHILDREN

Did I say my prayers without paying attention to them?

Did I omit my morning or night prayers?

Did I use God's name without respect or in anger?

Did I miss Mass on Sundays or Holy Days on purpose?

Did I misbehave, play or talk in church?

Did I treat holy things without reverence and respect?

Did I disobey my parents, teachers or those in authority?

Was I disrespectful to them?

Did I talk back to them?

Did I fight or argue with my brothers or sisters or others?

Did I get real angry?

Did I call anyone names?

Did I make fun of others?

Was I lazy?

Was I cruel to animals?

Did I give bad example?

Did I look at impure pictures?

Did I watch bad TV or movies?

Did I steal anything? Explain.

Did I break something that belonged to another?

Did I tell any lies?

Did I cheat?

Did I want what others have?

Was I jealous?

Did I eat meat on Friday on purpose?

Did I not go to confession at least once a year?

Did I make a bad confession by purposely leaving out
a mortal sin?

Did I not receive Holy Communion during the Easter time?

(Easter time lasts from Ash Wednesday until Trinity Sunday.)

If you honestly forgot to confess a mortal sin, the sin is forgiven and you may go to Holy Communion but you must confess the sin if it comes to mind again.

A Bad Confession

If you purposely conceal or leave out a mortal sin in confession, you commit a mortal sin of sacrilege and none of your sins are forgiven.

In order to have your sins forgiven if you made a bad confession you must:

- Tell the priest that you made a bad confession.

- Say the sin or sins you left out.

- Tell the priest the sacraments you received since then.

- Confess any other mortal sins, if you have committed any since your last good confession.

HOLY EUCHARIST

The sacrament that contains the Body, Blood, Soul and Divinity of Jesus Christ under the appearances of bread and wine is called the Holy Eucharist.

On Holy Thursday at the Last Supper, Jesus changed bread and wine into His Body and Blood. Christ gave this same power to the Apostles and to the bishops and priests who came after them.

During the Consecration of the Mass, the priest repeats the words and actions of Jesus at the Last Supper. The bread and wine are then changed into the Body and Blood of Christ. This miracle is called Transubstantiation.

When you go to church, you will see a candle inside a red glass on the left side of the altar. This candle is called the sanctuary lamp and it tells you that Jesus is in the tabernacle.

Jesus loves you so much that He stays in the Blessed Sacrament so you can visit Him and talk to Him.

When you receive Holy Communion, Jesus comes into your body and soul. Each Holy Communion is special and fills your soul with God's grace and love. Prepare your heart for Jesus by living a holy life and by saying your prayers every day. Ask Mary and your Guardian Angel to help you, too.

COMMUNION FAST

- You cannot have food or alcoholic beverages for three hours before you receive Holy Communion.
- You cannot drink anything for one hour.
- You may drink water and take necessary medicine any time before receiving Holy Communion.

When you receive Holy Communion, Jesus stays in your heart for about 15 minutes. Do not chew the Sacred Host. Swallow It as soon as it is moist enough to do so.

- If the Sacred Host sticks to the roof of your mouth, never touch It with your fingers, but use your tongue to help you swallow It.
- Never receive Holy Communion if you have a mortal sin on your soul. You must go to confession first. If you have venial sins on your soul, you can still go to Holy Communion.

31

- Never receive Holy Communion if you are sick and feel like throwing up.

- Do not receive Holy Communion if you have not kept the communion fast.

When the priest raises the Host and Chalice during the Consecration of the Mass you should look at the Sacred Host and Chalice and say: "My Lord and My God." Bells are rung to tell you that a great miracle has taken place and that Jesus is on the altar. After Holy Communion you can either say prayers on your own or read prayers from your missal. It is also good to say the Prayer before a Crucifix.

AT EACH HOLY COMMUNION

L-Tell Jesus you **love** Him & ask Him to help you always be good.

A-Ask Jesus to bless your family & friends.

S-Tell Jesus you are **sorry** for all your sins.

T-Thank Jesus for all He has done for you. **Talk** to Jesus.

PRAYERS AFTER HOLY COMMUNION

LOVE: Jesus, I love Thee with my whole heart and soul. I thank Thee for coming to me in Holy Communion today. I believe that Thou art in the Sacred Host. Thou art my best friend. Help me to always be good.

ASK: Dear Jesus, please bless and watch over me. Bless my mom and dad, my brothers and sisters, my grandparents, my cousins, my uncles and my aunts. Bless the priests and sisters who teach me how to love Thee and get to Heaven. Bless my teachers and my friends. Let me always be good and kind to everyone. Help me to obey Mom, Dad and my teachers and to always do my best. Let everyone in the world love Thee the way I do. Always keep me safe. Have mercy on the Souls in Purgatory so they can be with Thee in Heaven soon.

SORRY: Dear Jesus, I am so sorry for all my sins because they hurt Thee very much. Make me strong so I will always do what is right. Please help me be holy and pure. Give me grace to always be good and to resist the temptations of the devil.

THANK: Dear Jesus, Thou hast done so much for me. Thou hast died on the Cross for me and made Heaven so I can be happy with Thee forever. I thank Thee for creating such a beautiful world with lakes and seas, flowers and trees, mountains and hills, animals and birds, the sky and the sun, the moon and the stars. I thank Thee for my family. Bless us and help us get to Heaven. I thank Thee for making me a Catholic. I want to love Thee always. Please help me to always be a good example. Take me to Heaven when I die so I can be happy with Thee forever.

PRAYER BEFORE THE CRUCIFIX

Behold, O kind and most sweet Jesus, I cast myself upon my knees in Thy sight, and with the most fervent desire of my soul I pray and beseech Thee that Thou wouldst impress deep within my heart lively sentiments of faith, hope and charity, with true repentance for my sins and a firm purpose of amendment, whilst with deep affection and grief of soul I ponder within myself and mentally contemplate Thy five most precious Wounds; having before my eyes that which David in prophecy spoke concerning Thee, O Good Jesus: "They have pierced my hands and my feet; they have numbered all my bones."

Our Father... Hail Mary... Glory Be...

CONFIRMATION

The sacrament by which the Holy Ghost comes to you in a special way to help you practice your faith as a soldier of Jesus Christ is called Confirmation. The bishop confers the Sacrament of Confirmation.

HOLY OILS

Holy Oil—(OS Oleum Sanctum) is also called Oil of Catechumens. It is used for Baptism and Holy Orders.

Holy Chrism—(SC Sanctum Chrisma) is used for Baptism, Confirmation and the Consecration of a Bishop.

Oil of the Sick—(OI Oleum Infirmorum) is used for Extreme Unction.

As the bishop confirms you, he anoints you with Holy Chrism. This is a mixture of olive oil and balsam that he blessed on Holy Thursday.

While confirming you, the bishop says: "I sign thee with the sign of the cross and I confirm thee with the chrism of salvation in the name of the Father and of the Son and of the Holy Ghost."

In order to receive the Sacrament of Confirmation, you must be baptized, be in the state of grace (have no mortal sins on your soul) and know your faith.

Confirmation gives you an increase of sanctifying grace and the Seven Gifts of the Holy Ghost. It also strengthens your faith and Imprints a permanent seal on your soul.

Three sacraments put a permanent mark or character on your soul—Baptism, Confirmation and Holy Orders. They can be received only once.

The bishop gives a slight slap to the cheek of the person being confirmed in order to remind that person to live the Catholic Faith, be willing to suffer for the sake of Christ and if necessary, to die for Him.

When selecting a saint's name for Confirmation, it is important to choose a saint that you would like to model your life after. Your new patron saint will look after you from heaven.

The sponsor you choose for Confirmation must be a baptized and confirmed Catholic of the same gender as you.

THE SEVEN GIFTS OF THE HOLY GHOST

Wisdom—helps you see things the way God does.

Understanding—helps you tell truth from error.

Counsel—helps you make the right decision.

Fortitude—gives you the strength to do what is right.

Knowledge—helps you know God and yourself.

Piety—helps you to love God and your neighbor.

Fear of the Lord—helps you to love God so much that

you don't want to hurt Him.

12 Fruits of the Holy Ghost

Charity, Joy,

Peace, Patience,

Goodness, Kindness (Benignity),

Mildness, Modesty,

Chastity, Continency,

Long Suffering and Faith.

Matrimony

The sacrament that unites a baptized man and woman for life in marriage and gives them all the graces they need is called Matrimony.

Holy Orders

The sacrament that gives men the power and grace to be bishops, priests and other ministers of the Church is called Holy Orders. There are numerous steps to the priesthood: tonsure, porter, lector, exorcist, acolyte, subdeacon, deacon and priest. The bishop possesses the fullness of the priesthood.

EXTREME UNCTION

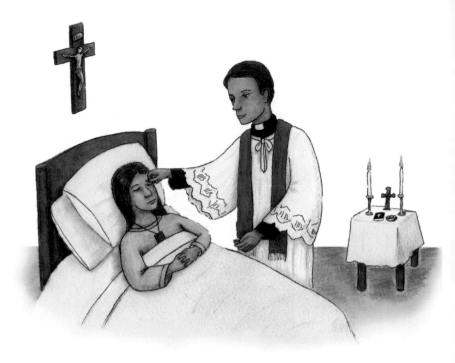

The sacrament that gives health and strength to the soul and sometimes to the body when you are in danger of death is called Extreme Unction.

THE HOLY SACRIFICE OF THE MASS

Offertory—Bread and wine are offered to God.

Consecration—Bread and wine are changed into

the Body, Blood, Soul and Divinity of Jesus Christ.

Communion—You receive Jesus.

The Holy Sacrifice of the Mass is a renewal in an unbloody manner of the Sacrifice of the Cross. The three main parts of the Mass are the Offertory, Consecration and Communion.

VESTMENTS USED FOR MASS

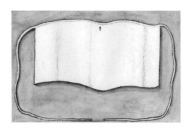

Amice—a rectangular linen cloth with two strings that is worn over the priest's shoulders. The amice represents the blindfold used to cover Jesus' eyes during the Passion.

Alb—a long white garment worn by the priest. It symbolizes the white robe of mockery that Herod placed on Jesus during His Passion. (The word "alb" is derived from the Latin word for white.)

Cincture—a cord worn around the waist that is usually the same color as the outer vestment. It symbolizes the scourges that were used to torture Jesus.

Maniple—a short narrow piece of silk, velvet or other colored material with a cross at the top and on the lower portion of both sides that is worn over the left arm. It symbolizes the ropes by which Jesus was led during the Passion.

Stole—a long narrow piece of fabric with a cross at the top and on the bottom of both sides that is worn around the neck. It symbolizes the rope that tied Jesus to the pillar. It is worn by the priest in the administration of all the sacraments.

Chasuble—a large colored garment worn over the other vestments. It symbolizes Jesus' purple robe of scorn. (The word chasuble is derived from the Latin word for little house.)

Gothic Style
long flowing garment that drapes over the arms.

Roman Style
stiff garment that hangs in the front and back.

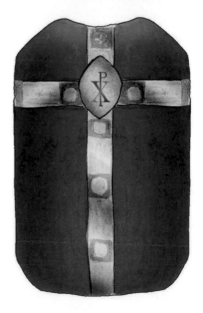

Tunic—sleeved garment worn by the subdeacon during Solemn High Mass.

Dalmatic—sleeved garment worn by the deacon during Solemn High Mass.

KINDS OF MASSES

Two candles are lit for a normal daily Mass **(Low Mass)**. Six candles are lit for a **Sung** or **High Mass (Missa Cantata)**. During a **Solemn High Mass** the priest is assisted by a deacon and subdeacon. A **Requiem Mass** is a Mass offered for the Faithful Departed. A **Nuptial Mass** is offered when the Sacrament of Matrimony takes place. A **Votive Mass** is offered for a special intention.

Liturgical Colors

White: Worn on feasts of Christ, Mary, angels, and saints who were not martyrs and for Nuptial Masses.

Red: Masses of the Holy Ghost (the week of Pentecost and Votive Masses), feasts in honor of the Passion and the Cross and for martyrs (those who shed their blood for Christ).

Gold: Christmas, Easter and major feasts. It can also be used in place of white, red or green.

Green: Sundays after Epiphany and Pentecost.

Rose: Gaudete Sunday (Advent) and Laetare Sunday (Lent).

Violet: Advent, Septuagesima, Lent, Passiontide, Vigils, Rogation Days and most Ember Days.

Black: Masses for the Dead (Requiem Masses) and Funerals.

Liturgical Seasons

Advent: The Four Sundays before Christmas.

Christmas: December 25, Christ's birthday.

Epiphany: January 6, the Three Kings adore Jesus.

Sundays After Epiphany

Septuagesima: The three Sundays before Lent begins.

Lent: The 40 day period from Ash Wednesday until Easter. There are four Sundays of Lent before Passiontide.

Passiontide: The two Sundays before Easter. This season includes Passion Sunday, Palm Sunday and Holy Week.

Easter: Jesus rises from the dead.

Sundays after Easter

Pentecost: The Holy Ghost descends upon Mary and the Apostles.

Sundays after Pentecost: The remaining Sundays of the year.

LITURGICAL BOOKS

Roman Missal—altar missal used by the priest during Mass.

Roman Ritual—book of blessings and exorcisms.

Roman Breviary—contains the Divine Office—the 150 psalms of King David, scriptural readings and writings from the saints. The priest recites the Divine Office every day.

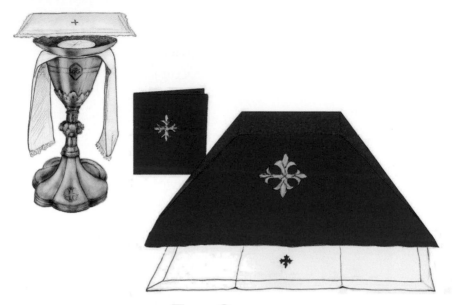

THE CHALICE

The **chalice** is a gold plated cup. A **purificator** drapes over it. This linen has three folds and a red cross on the top. It is used to purify the chalice. The **paten** is a gold covered plate on which the host rests. A stiff piece of square linen called the **pall** rests on the top of the chalice. It protects the chalice from foreign objects. The **chalice veil** drapes over the chalice until the Offertory. The chalice is covered again after Communion. The **burse** is the two-piece square cloth that opens and contains a **corporal**. The corporal is a square piece of linen on which the chalice and host rest during Mass. It has a red cross sewn in the front or the middle. The **chalice veil** and **burse** are the same color as the vestment worn by the priest.

Ciborium: a gold container that holds consecrated Hosts.

Pyx: a gold plated object used to bring Hosts to the sick.

Burse: a leather case that holds the pyx and is worn around the priest's neck during sick calls.

Cruets—glass containers that hold water and wine for Mass.

Lavabo Dish—a glass dish used when washing the priest's hands.

Paten—a gold plated dish placed under the chin at Communion.

Bells—inform the faithful of the solemn parts of the Mass.

Biretta—a black hat worn by the priest to and from the altar.

Aspergel / Aspersorium—holy water sprinkler and bucket.

ITEMS USED FOR BENEDICTION

Cope: long clasped cape used for Processions and Benediction.

Humeral Veil: long narrow garment worn over the shoulders for Benediction. The priest uses it to hold the monstrance.

Monstrance: a large gold plated sacred vessel that holds the Sacred Host.

Luna: a circular crystal container that holds the Sacred Host.

Capsula: a container that holds the luna.

Censer: charcoal burner used for Benediction and processions.

Boat: holds incense.

Candelabra: candleholder.

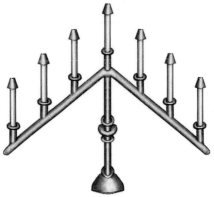

Ablution Bowl: used to purify the priest's fingers after the distribution of Holy Communion.

THE CHURCH

The front of the church is called the **sanctuary**. A red candle, the **sanctuary lamp**, burns on the side of the altar to show that the Blessed Sacrament is present. The **altar** rests on a platform. The marble **altar stone** in the center of the altar contains relics of two martyrs. It has five crosses etched on its surface symbolizing the Five Wounds of Jesus. The **tabernacle** is a safe made of brass or wood that rests on the altar and holds the Sacred Hosts that are kept in the ciborium. A **crucifix** always hangs above the altar or rests on top of the tabernacle. The sanctuary is separated from the body of the church by the **communion rail** which usually has a linen cloth draped over it. The **ambry**, located on the right wall of the sanctuary, houses the Holy Oils.

THE HOLY SACRIFICE OF THE MASS AND THE PASSION OF CHRIST

The ceremonies of the Holy Sacrifice of the Mass represent the various events that took place during Christ's Passion, Death and Resurrection.

The Priest goes to the Altar:

Jesus goes to the Garden of Olives (Gethsemane). Stand.

The Prayers at the Foot of the Altar:

Jesus foresees His terrible sufferings and the sins of the world. He prays and sweats blood while the Apostles sleep. (Priest and servers bow low.) Kneel.

The Priest kisses the Altar: Jesus is betrayed by Judas' kiss.

Introit: Jesus is brought before Annas and is struck by one of the attendants.

Kyrie Eleison: St. Peter denies Jesus three times. The *Kyrie* is the only prayer in the Mass recited in the Greek language.

Gloria: Jesus is brought before the high priest, Caiphas.

Dominus Vobiscum: Jesus looks at Peter.

Epistle: Jesus is led to the Roman governor, Pontius Pilate, and accused by false witnesses. Sit or kneel.

Gospel: Jesus is mocked by Herod. The Sign of the Cross is made three times: once on the forehead, lips and over the heart. This action asks God that we understand the teachings of the Gospel with our mind, it be spoken from our lips and that we may always love Him with our heart. Stand.

Creed: Jesus is mocked by the soldiers and crowd. Stand.

Offertory: Jesus is scourged. Sit.

The priest offers the chalice and covers it. Jesus is crowned with thorns and clothed in a purple cloak.

Washing of the Hands: Pontius Pilate washes his hands.

Orate Fratres: Jesus is presented before the people.

Preface / Sanctus: Jesus is condemned to death while the crowd cries, "crucify Him!" three times. (The bells are rung three times.) Kneel.

Canon of the Mass: Jesus carries the Cross, is met by His Blessed Mother and falls several times. Veronica wipes the Sacred Face of Jesus. (The priest prays very quietly.) The word "Canon" is derived from the Greek word meaning "fixed rule."

Hanc Igitur: When Jesus arrives on Calvary, He is stripped of His garments and crucified. The priest places his hands over the host and chalice while his thumbs form a cross. The bells ring once. This imposition of hands signifies that Christ died for the sins of the world on the Cross.

Quam Oblationem: Jesus is nailed to the Cross.

Consecration: The priest reenacts the miracle of the Last Supper when he, in the person of Christ, repeats the words and actions of Our Lord. The substance of the bread and wine are changed into the Body, Blood, Soul and Divinity of Jesus Christ. This miracle is called Transubstantiation. There are separate consecrations of the host and wine to represent the Sacrifice of the Cross—when Jesus', dying on the Cross, shed His Blood for our redemption.

Elevation: Jesus is raised on the Cross and His Precious Blood flows from His wounds. Pope St. Gregory X began the practice of elevating the Host and Chalice during the Canon of the Mass to outwardly manifest belief in the Real Presence of Christ in the Holy Eucharist. The bells are rung three times to inform the faithful that the Consecration of the Host and Chalice have taken place. It is customary for the faithful to say quietly "My Lord and My God."

Remaining Prayers of the Canon / Our Father: The Seven Last Words spoken by Christ from the Cross.

The Host is broken: Jesus dies upon the Cross.

A Particle of the Host is placed in the Chalice: Jesus Sacred Body is taken down from the Cross and His soul descends into Limbo.

Agnus Dei: St. Longinus pierces Our Lord's Sacred Heart with a lance and proclaims His Divinity.

Priest's Communion / The Communion of the Faithful: Jesus is laid in the tomb.

Prayers after Communion: Jesus rises from the dead.

Ite Missa Est: Jesus ascends into Heaven.

The Priest Gives his Blessing: The Descent of the Holy Ghost at Pentecost. It is customary to always kneel for a priest's blessing.

Last Gospel: The Gospel is preached throughout the world. Stand.

THE 15 MYSTERIES OF THE ROSARY

The Blessed Virgin Mary appeared to St. Dominic in 1214 **AD** and taught him the Joyful, Sorrowful and Glorious Mysteries of the Rosary.

Joyful Mysteries are prayed on Mondays, Thursdays and on the Sundays of Advent, Christmas, Epiphany and Septuagesima.

Sorrowful Mysteries are prayed on Tuesdays, Fridays and on the Sundays of Lent.

Glorious Mysteries are prayed on Wednesdays, Saturdays and on the Sundays of Easter and Pentecost.

When you pray the Rosary you do two different things:

(1) Move your fingers along the beads as you say the Apostles' Creed, the Our Father, the Hail Mary and the Glory Be.

(2) At the same time, you meditate on (think about) the joys, sorrows and glories of Jesus and Mary.

JOYFUL MYSTERIES

THE ANNUNCIATION

The Angel Gabriel announces to Mary that she is to become the Mother of God.

THE VISITATION

Mary visits her cousin St. Elizabeth.

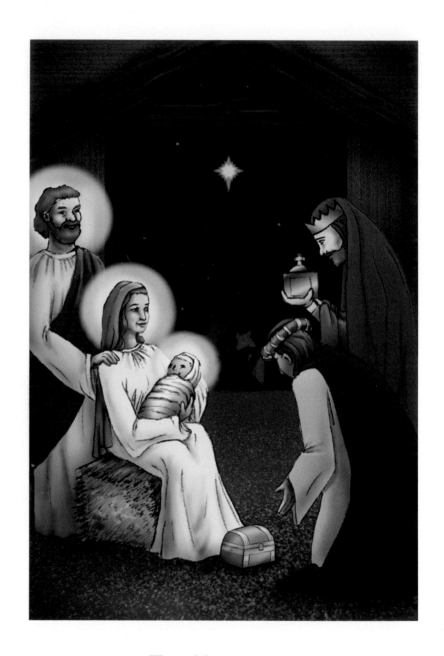

THE NATIVITY

Jesus is born in Bethlehem.

THE PRESENTATION

Jesus is presented in the Temple.

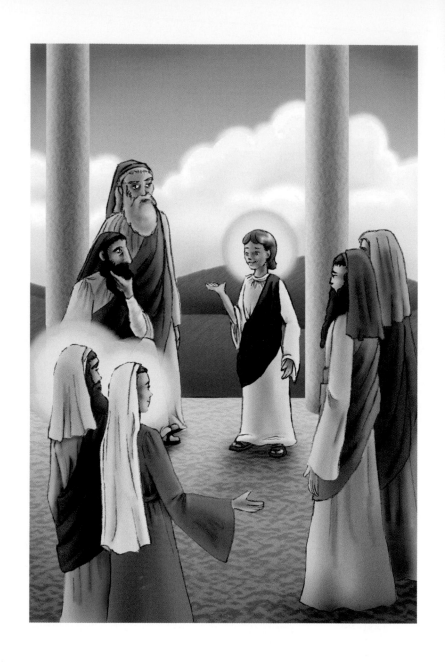

THE FINDING IN THE TEMPLE

Jesus is found in the Temple in Jerusalem

after three days.

Sorrowful Mysteries

The Agony in the Garden

Jesus sweats blood as He sees the sins of the world and

the sufferings He will go through during the Passion.

THE SCOURGING AT THE PILLAR

Jesus is whipped by the soldiers for our sins.

THE CROWNING WITH THORNS

Soldiers cruelly press a crown of sharp thorns

onto Jesus' head.

THE CARRYING OF THE CROSS

Jesus lovingly carries His heavy cross to Calvary

THE CRUCIFIXION

Jesus dies on the Cross to make up for the sins

of the world and to open the gates of Heaven.

GLORIOUS MYSTERIES

THE RESURRECTION

Jesus rises from the dead on Easter morning.

THE ASCENSION

Jesus ascends into Heaven by His own power.

THE DESCENT OF THE HOLY GHOST

The Holy Ghost descends upon Mary and the Apostles.

THE ASSUMPTION

Mary is assumed into Heaven.

THE CORONATION

Mary is crowned Queen of Heaven

and earth, angels and saints.

The Stations of the Cross

During the Stations of the Cross, you retrace the steps that Jesus took as He suffered and died for you.

I. Jesus is Condemned to Death

Jesus, help me to be brave and always do what God asks. I thank Thee for coming on earth to die for me.

II. Jesus Takes Up the Cross

Jesus help me never to complain when I am told to do something difficult. I will carry my cross and follow Thee.

III. Jesus Falls the First Time

Jesus help me to be strong and never give up when it's hard to live my faith. I will always love Thee.

IV. Jesus Meets His Blessed Mother

Mary help me to always be good and to never sin again. Please lead me to Heaven.

V. Simon of Cyrene Helps Jesus Carry the Cross

Jesus help me to always be kind. I will assist others whenever I can.

VI. VERONICA WIPES THE FACE OF JESUS

Jesus let me remember that every time I help others I show my love for Thee. I will try to be kind to everyone for love of Thee.

VII. Jesus Falls the Second Time

Jesus, I am very weak. Please help me to be sorry for my sins, change my life and make a good confession.

VIII. Jesus Speaks to the Women of Jerusalem

Jesus teach me the way to Heaven and give me the grace to love Thee more and more each day. I am sorry for all my sins.

IX. Jesus Falls the Third Time

Jesus give me the strength to keep going and to always do what is right. With Thy help I will try to never sin again.

X. Jesus is Stripped of His Garments

Jesus I will stay away from bad people who lead me away from Thee. I want to always love Thee.

XI. Jesus is Nailed to the Cross

Let me always remember that it was my sins that nailed Thee to the Cross. I will try never to hurt Thee by my sins again.

XII. Jesus Dies on the Cross

Jesus, I thank Thee for suffering and dying for me on the Cross in order to open the gates of Heaven. I love Thee very much.

XIII. Jesus is Taken Down from the Cross

Mary, keep me close to Jesus. Please help me be holy so that I never sin again.

XIV. JESUS IS LAID IN THE TOMB

Jesus, keep me safe and protect me on earth so I can live with Thee forever in Heaven. Amen.

To gain a Plenary Indulgence for saying the Stations of the Cross, pray one Our Father, one Hail Mary and one Glory Be.

THE TWELVE APOSTLES

- St. Peter

- St. Andrew

- St. James the Greater

- St. John

- St. Philip

- St. Bartholomew

- St. Thomas

- St. Matthew

- St. James the Less

- St. Jude Thaddeus

- St. Simon the Cananean

- Judas Iscariot betrayed Jesus. He was replaced by

- St. Matthias

Saints Peter and Andrew were brothers.

Saints James the Greater and John were also brothers.

Saints James the Less, Jude Thaddeus and Simon were cousins of Jesus.

THE FOUR EVANGELISTS
WHO WROTE THE GOSPELS

St. Matthew's Gospel begins with the
genealogy (family tree) of Jesus.
His symbol is an angel or a man.

St. Mark's Gospel opens with the
story of St. John the Baptist in the
wilderness. His symbol is a lion.

St. Luke's Gospel begins with Zachary
offering sacrifice in the temple.
His symbol is an ox.

The first chapter of the Gospel
of St. John soars heavenward
by proclaiming the Divinity of Christ.
His symbol is an eagle.

Proofs for the Existence of God

Law

Laws, necessary to maintain order and to preserve the common good, are found in every culture. This tells us that there has to be an ultimate Lawgiver: Almighty God. The Natural Law, upon which the Ten Commandments are based, includes our duties to God and our neighbor. All are bound to obey Natural Law in order to achieve happiness and maintain right order in society. Our conscience helps us distinguish between right and wrong. All people have a conscience and are ultimately responsible to Almighty God for their actions, yet consciences can also become hardened or stifled.

Effect

No living thing gives itself life. Everything must have a cause for its existence. Yet there had to be a Being who had no beginning—who created the world around us. God is this First Cause. He had no beginning and will have no end. God is uncaused and has always existed.

Order

There is a harmony in the universe—an orderly arrangement made to serve a definite purpose. Consider the wonderful variety and multitude of species, the cycles of night and day, the timeliness of seasons, tides, the systematic alignment and orbit of planets, all guided intelligently by an infinite, Supreme Being—Almighty God.

Greek Abbreviations Used in Church

IHS is an abbreviation of the word Jesus (ΙΗΣΟΥΣ).

☧ is an abbreviation of the word Christ (ΧΡΙΣΤΟΣ).

A Ω The Alpha and Omega are the first and last letters of the Greek alphabet. The symbols A Ω beautifully symbolize that God always was and always will be.

Review

Who is God?

God is the Supreme Being who made all things. God is infinitely good, infinitely perfect and almighty.

Explain the Blessed Trinity.

There are Three Persons in One God: Father, Son and Holy Ghost. This is called the Blessed Trinity.

Why did God make you?

God made you to know, love and serve Him in this world so you can be happy with Him forever in Heaven.

What is the Mass?

The Holy Sacrifice of the Mass is a renewal in an unbloody manner of the Sacrifice of the Cross.

What are the Four Marks of the Church?

One: The same Mass, Sacraments and teachings.

Holy: Christ, who is all holy, founded the Catholic Church.
It teaches holy doctrines and has the means of holiness,
the Mass and the sacraments.

Catholic: It is Universal—the same Church all over the world.
The Catholic Church teaches all the truths revealed
by God to all nations of the world.

Apostolic: Christ founded the Church on the 12 Apostles.
Their successors are the Catholic bishops.

What is a Sacrament?

A Sacrament is an outward sign, instituted by Christ, to give grace.

Name the Seven Sacraments.

Baptism, Penance, Holy Eucharist, Confirmation, Matrimony, Holy Orders and Extreme Unction.

Which sacraments put an indelible mark on your soul?

Baptism, Confirmation and Holy Orders.

What must you do if you commit a mortal sin?

If you commit a mortal sin, you should immediately pray the Act of Contrition and go to Confession as soon as possible.

What is a mortal sin?

A mortal sin is a serious offence against the law of God. If you die with an unforgiven mortal sin on your soul, you will go to Hell.

What three conditions make a sin mortal?

1) It must be seriously wrong or considered seriously wrong.

2) You must know that it is seriously wrong.

3) You do it anyway. You give full consent.

What are the three major parts of the Mass?

Offertory, Consecration and Communion.

SERVER RESPONSES AT MASS

PRAYERS AT THE FOOT OF THE ALTAR

Priest: + *In nomine Patris et Filii et Spiritus Sancti.*
Amen. Introíbo ad altáre Dei.

Server: Ad Deum qui laetíficat júventutem meam.

[Ahd day-oom kwee lay-tee-fee-cot you-ven-too-tem
may-ahm]

P: *Júdica me, Deus, et discérne causam meam, de gente*
non sancta: ab hómine iníquo et dolóso erue me.

S: Quia tu es, Deus, fortitúdo mea: quare me repulísti, et
quare tristis incédo, dum afflígit me inimícus?

[Kwee-ah too es day-oos for-tee-too-doe may-ah kwar-
ray may ray-pool-lee-stee et kwar-ray tree-stees in-
chay-doe doom ah-flee-jeet may ih-nee-me-coos]

P: *Emítte tuum et veritátem tuam: Ipsa me deduxérunt et*
adduxérunt in montem sanctum tuum et in tabernácula
tua.

S: Et introibo ad altare Dei: ad Deum qui laetificat
juventútem meam.

[Et intro-ee-bow ahd all-tar-ray day-ee ahd day-oom
kwee lay-tee-fee-cot you-ven-too-tem may-ahm]

97

P: *Confitébor tibi in cíthara, Deus, Deus meus: quare tristis es ánima mea, et quare contúrbas me.*

S: Spera in Deo quóniam adhuc confitébor illi: salutáre vultus mei, et Deus meus.

[Spay-rah in day-oh kwoh-knee-ohm ahd-hook cohn-fee-tay-bor ee-lee sa-loo-tah-ray vul-toos-ss may-ee et day-oos may-oos]

P: *Glória Patri, et Fílio, et Spirítui Sancto.*

S: Sicut erat in princípio, et nunc, et semper: et in saécula saeculórum. Amen.

[See-coot ay-rot in prin-chee-pee-oh et noonk et sem-pair et in say-coo-la say-coo-loh-room ah-men]

P: *Introíbo ad altáre Dei.*

S: Ad Deum qui laetíficat juventútem meam.

[Ahd day-uhm kwee lay-tee-fee-cot you-ven-too-tem may-ahm]

P: + *Adjutórium nostrum in nómine Dómini.*

S: Qui fecit caelum et terram.

[Kwee fay-cheat chay-loom et tayr-rahm]

The priest says the Confiteor.

Once the Confiteor is finished,
the Server says:

S: Misereátur tui omnípotens Deus et dímissis peccátis tuis perdúcat te ad vitam aetérnam. P: Amen.

[Me-zay-ree-ah-tour too-ee ohm-knee-poh-tens day-oos et dee-me-sees pay-ca-tees too-ees pair-doo-cot tay ahd vee-tom ay-tair-nam.] P: Ahmen.

S: Confiteor Deo omnipoténti, beátae Maríae semper Vírgini, beáto Michaéli Archángelo, beáto Joánni Baptístae, sanctis Apostolis Petro et Paulo, omnibus Sanctis, et tibi pater, quia peccavi nimis cogitatione, verbo, et opere: mea culpa, mea culpa, mea maxima culpa. Ideo precor beatam Mariam semper Virginem, beatum Michaelem Archangelum, beatum Joannem Baptistam, sanctos Apostolos Petrum et Paulum, omnes Sanctos, et te, pater, orare pro me ad Dominum Deum nostrum.

[Con-fee-tay-or day-oh ohm-knee-poe-ten-tee bay-ah-tay ma-ree-aa sem-pair veer-geen-knee bay-ah-toe me-ca-ay-lee ark-ahn-jay-low bay-ah-toe yo-ahn-knee bap-tees-tay sahnk-tees a-poh-stoh-lees pay-tro et pow-lo ohm-knee-boos sanc-tees et tee-bee pa-tair kwee-ah pay-cah-vee knee-mees coh-gee-tot-see-oh-nay vair-bow et oh-pay-ray may-ah cool-pa, may-ah cool-pa, may-ah mahk-see-mah cool-pah, ee-day-oh pray-cor bay-ah-tom ma-ree-ahm sem-pair veer-jen-nem bay-ah-tum me-ca-ay-lem ark-ahn-gel-oom bay-ah-tum yo-ah-nem bahp-tee-stahm sahnk-tohs ah-pah-sto-lohs pay-trum et paw-lum ohm-nays sahnk-tohs et tay pah-tair oh-rah-ray pro may ahd doe-mee-noom day-oom noh-stroom]

P: Misereatur vestri, etc.

S: Amen. [Ah-men]

P: + Indulgentiam, absolutionem, etc.

S: Amen. [Ah-men]

P: Deus, tu conversus vivificabis nos.

S: Et plebs tua laetabitur in te.

   [Et playbs too-ah lay-tah-bee-tour in tay]

P: Ostende nobis, Domine, misericordiam tuam.

S: Et salutare tuum da nobis.

[Et sa-loo-tah-ray too-oohm dah no-beess]

P: Domine, exaudi orationem meam.

S: Et clamor meus ad te veniat.

[Et clah-mor may-oos ahd tay vay-knee-aht]

P: Dominus vobiscum.

S: Et cum spiritu tuo. [Et coom spee-ree-too to-ooh]

P: Oremus

THE PRIEST THEN ASCENDS TO THE ALTAR.

P: Kyrie eleison

S: Kyrie eleison [Kee-ree-ay ay-lay-ee-sohn]

P: Kyrie eleison

S: Christe eleison [Cree-stay ay-lay-ee-sohn]

P: Christe eleison

S: Christe eleison [Cree-stay ay-lay-ee-sohn]

P: Kyrie eleison

S: Kyrie eleison [Kee-ree-ay ay-lay-ee-sohn]

P: Kyrie eleison

THE PRIEST TURNS TOWARD THE PEOPLE AND SAYS:

P: Dominus vobiscum.

S: Et cum spiritu tuo. [Et coom spee-ree-too to-ooh]

THE PRIEST FINISHES THE PRAYER AND SAYS:

P: Per omnia saecula saeculorum.

S: Amen. [Ah-men]

WHEN THE EPISTLE IS FINISHED, SAY:

S: Deo gratias. [Day-oh grah-tsee-ahs]

AT THE GOSPEL, THE PRIEST SAYS:

P: Dominus vobiscum.

S: Et cum spiritu tuo. [Et coom spee-ree-too to-ooh]

P: Sequentia...

S: Gloria tibi Domine. [Gloh-ree-ah tee-bee doe-mee-nay]

AT THE END OF THE GOSPEL, SAY:

S: Laus tibi, Christe. [Laus tee-bee cree-stay]

AT THE OFFERTORY, THE PRIEST SAYS:

P: Dominus vobiscum.

S: Et cum spiritu tuo. [Et coom spee-ree-too to-ooh]

WHEN YOU RETURN TO YOUR PLACE AFTER WASHING THE PRIEST'S HANDS, THE PRIEST SAYS:

P: Orate fratres...

S: Suscipiat Dominus sacrificium de manibus tuis, ad laudem et gloriam nominis sui, ad utilitatem quoque nostrum, totiusque ecclesiae suae sanctae.

[Soo-shee-pee-aht doe-mee-noos sah-crah-fee-chee-oom day mah-knee-boos too-ees ahd loud-dem et gloh-ree-ahm noh-mee-nee soo-ee ahd oo-tee-lee-tah-tem kwoh-kway noh-strum toht-see-oos-kway ay-clay-zee-ay soo-ay sahnk-tay]

AT THE END OF THE SECRET, THE PRIEST SAYS:

P: Per omnia saecula saeculorum.

S: Amen. [Ah-men]

AT THE PREFACE, THE PRIEST SAYS:

P: Dominus vobiscum.

S: Et cum spiritu tuo. [Et coom spee-ree-too to-ooh]

P: Sursum corda.

S: Habemus ad Dominum.

   [Ah-bay-moose ahd doe-me-noom]

P: Gratias agamus Domino Deo nostro.

S: Dignum et justum est. [Dee-nyoom et you-stoom est]

AFTER THE MINOR ELEVATION, THE PRIEST SAYS:

P: Per omnia saecula saeculorum.

S: Amen. [Ah-men]

AT THE END OF THE OUR FATHER, THE PRIEST SAYS:

P: Et ne nos inducas in tentationem.

S: Sed libera nos a malo.

   [Sed le bay-rah nohs ah mah-low]

AFTER THE BREAKING OF THE HOST, THE PRIEST SAYS:

P: Per omnia saecula saeculorum.

S: Amen. [Ah-men]

P: Pax Domini sit semper vobiscum.

S: Et cum spiritu tuo. [Et coom spee-ree-too to-ooh]

WHEN THE PRIEST OPENS THE TABERNACLE DOOR, SAY THE CONFITEOR.

S: Confiteor Deo omnipoténti, beátae Maríae semper Vírgini, beáto Michaéli Archángelo, beáto Joánni Baptístae, sanctis Apostolis Petro et Paulo, omnibus Sanctis, et tibi pater, quia peccavi nimis cogitatione, verbo, et opere: mea culpa, mea culpa, mea maxima culpa. Ideo precor beatam Mariam semper Virginem, beatum Michaelem Archangelum, beatum Joannem Baptistam, sanctos Apostolos Petrum et Paulum, omnes Sanctos, et te, pater, orare pro me ad Dominum Deum nostrum.

[Con-fee-tay-or day-oh ohm-knee-poe-ten-tee bay-ah-tay ma-ree-aa sem-pair veer-geen-knee bay-ah-toe me-ca-ay-lee ark-ahn-jay-low bay-ah-toe yo-ahn-knee bap-tees-tay sahnk-tees a-poh-stoh-lees pay-tro et pow-lo ohm-knee-boos sanc-tees et tee-bee pa-tair kwee-ah pay-cah-vee knee-mees coh-gee-tot-see-oh-nay vair-bow et oh-pay-ray may-ah cool-pa, may-ah cool-pa, may-ah mahk-see-mah cool-pah, ee-day-oh pray-cor bay-ah-tom ma-ree-ahm sem-pair veer-jen-nem bay-ah-tum me-ca-ay-loom ark-ahn-gel-em bay-ah-tum yo-ah-nem bahp-tee-stahm sahnk-tohs ah-pah-sto-lohs pay-trum et paw-lum ohm-nays sahnk-tohs et tay pah-tair oh-rah-ray pro may ahd doe-mee-noom day-oom noh-stroom]

P: Misereatur vestri, etc.

S: Amen. [Ah-men]

P: + Indulgentiam, absolutionem, etc.

S: Amen. [Ah-men]

AFTER THE COMMUNION VERSE, THE PRIEST SAYS:

P: Dominus vobiscum.

S: Et cum spiritu tuo. [Et coom spee-ree-too to-ooh]

AT THE POSTCOMMUNION, THE PRIEST SAYS:

P: Per omnia saecula saeculorum.

S: Amen. [Ah-men]

AFTER THE POSTCOMMUNION, THE PRIEST SAYS:

P: Dominus vobiscum.

S: Et cum spiritu tuo. [Et coom spee-ree-too to-ooh]

P: Ite missa est.

S: Deo gratias. [Day-oh grah-tsee-ahs]

For Masses where there is no Gloria—Advent, Lent, Weddings, Ferial Masses and Most Votive Masses:

P: Benedicamus Domino.

S: Deo gratias. [Day-oh grah-tsee-ahs]

For Requiem Masses and Funerals:

P: Requiescant in Pace.

S: Amen. [Ah-men]

AT THE BLESSING:

P: + Benedícat vos omnípotens Deus,

Pater, et Fílius et Spíritus Sanctus.

S: Amen. [Ah-men]

AT THE BEGINNING OF THE LAST GOSPEL, THE PRIEST SAYS:

P: Dominus vobiscum.

S: Et cum spiritu tuo.

[Et coom spee-ree-too to-ooh]

AFTER THE LAST GOSPEL, SAY:

S: Deo gratias. [Day-oh grah-tsee-ahs]

SURPLICE

CASSOCK

CATHOLIC HYMNS

O Salutaris Hostia

O salutaris Hostia, Quae coeli pandis ostium:

Bella premunt hostilia, Da robur, fer auxilium.

Uni trinoque Domino Sit sempiterna gloria!

Qui vitam sine termino, Nobis donet in patria. Amen.

Tantum Ergo

Tantum ergo Sacramentum Veneremur cernui,

Et antiquum documentum Novo cedat ritui.

Praestet fides supplementum, Sensuum defectui.

Genitori, Genitoque Laus et jubilatio,

Salus, honor, virtus quoque, Sit et benedictio.

Procedenti ab utroque, Compar sit laudatio. Amen.

Holy God

Holy God, we praise Thy Name! Lord of all, we bow before Thee.

All on earth Thy sceptre claim, All in Heav'n above adore Thee:

Infinite Thy vast domain, Everlasting is Thy reign. (Repeat)

Hark! the loud celestial hymn, Angel choirs above are raising!

Cherubim and Seraphim, In unceasing chorus praising.

Fill the Heaven's with sweet accord; Holy, holy, holy Lord.

(Repeat)

God Father Praise and Glory

God Father, praise and glory Thy children bring to Thee.

Good will and peace to mankind Shall now forever be.

Chorus: O most Holy Trinity, Undivided Unity;

Holy God, Mighty God, God Immortal, be adored.

And Thou, Lord Co-eternal, God's sole begotten Son;

O Jesus, King anointed, Who hast redemption won. (Chorus.)

O Holy Ghost, Creator, Thou Gift of God most high;

Life, love, and sacred Unction, our weakness Thou supply.

(Chorus.)

Jesus My Lord My God My All

Jesus, my Lord, my God, my All!

How can I love Thee as I ought?

And how revere this wondrous Gift,

So far surpassing hope or thought.

Chorus: Sweet Sacrament! we Thee adore!

Oh make us love thee more and more.

Oh! make us love Thee more and more.

Had I but Mary's sinless heart.

To love thee with my dearest King!

Oh with what bursts of fervent praise

Thy goodness, Jesus, would I sing! (Chorus.)

Come Holy Ghost

Come, Holy Ghost, Creator blest,

And in our hearts take up Thy rest;

Come with Thy grace and heavenly aid.

To fill the hearts which Thou hast made.

To fill the hearts which Thou hast made.

O Comforter to Thee we cry,

Thou heavenly Gift of God Most High.

Thou Fount of life and fire of love,

And sweet anointing from above.

And sweet anointing from above.

Praise to the Lord

Praise to the Lord, The Almighty the King of creation.

Oh my soul praise Him for He is your health and salvation.

All you who hear, now to His altar draw near,

Join in profound adoration.

Praise to the Lord, Oh, let all that is in us adore Him.

All that has life and breath come now in praises before Him.

Let the amen, sound from His people again.

Now as we worship before Him.

Bring Flowers of the Rarest

Bring flowers of the rarest, Bring flowers of the fairest.

From garden and woodland and hillside and vale;

Our full hearts are swelling, Our glad voices telling.

The praise of the loveliest rose of the dale.

Chorus: O Mary! we crown thee with blossoms today,

Queen of the angels, Queen of the May.

O Mary! we crown thee with blossoms today,

Queen of the Angels, Queen of the May.

Our voices ascending in harmony blending.

Oh thus may our hearts turn, dear Mother to thee:

Oh! thus shall we prove thee how truly we love thee,

How dark without Mary life's journey would be.

(Chorus.)

O Sanctissima

O Sanctissima, O piissima, Dulcis Virgo Maria!

Mater amata, Intemerata, Ora, Ora pro nobis.

Tu solatium Et refugium Virgo Mater Maria!

Quidquid optamus, Per te speramus; Ora, ora pro nobis.

On This Day, O Beautiful Mother

On this day, O beautiful Mother,

On this day we give thee our love.

Near thee, Madonna, fondly we hover,

Trusting thy gentle care to prove.

Chorus: On this day we ask to share,

Dearest Mother, thy sweet care;

Aid us ere our feet astray

Wander from thy guiding way.

Queen of angels, deign to hear

Lisping children's humble pray'r;

Young hearts gain, O Virgin pure,

Sweetly to thyself allure. (Chorus.)

'Tis the Month of Our Mother

'Tis the month of our Mother,

The blessed and beautiful days,

When our lips and our spirits

Are glowing with love and with praise.

Chorus: All hail! to dear Mary,

The guardian of our way,

To the fairest of all Queens,

Be the fairest of seasons, sweet May.

Hail Holy Queen

Hail, holy Queen, enthron'd above, O Maria!

Hail Mother of Mercy and of love, O Maria!

Chorus: Triumph, all ye Cherubim,

Sing with us, ye Seraphim.

Heav'n and earth resound the hymn:

Salve, salve, salve Regina!

Our life, our sweetness here below, O Maria!

Our hope in sorrow and in woe, O Maria! (Chorus.)

Sing of Mary

Sing of Mary, pure and lowly, Virgin mother undefiled,

Sing of God's own Son most holy,

Who became her little Child.

Fairest Child of fairest mother,

God, the Lord, who came to earth,

Word-made-flesh, our very Brother,

Takes our nature by His birth.

Sing of Jesus, Son of Mary, In the home at Nazareth.

Toil and labor cannot weary, Love enduring unto death.

Constant was the love He gave her,

Though He went forth from her side,

Forth to preach and heal and suffer,

Till on Calvary He died.

O Come, O Come, Emmanuel

O come, O come, Emmanuel!

And ransom captive Israel,

That mourns in lonely exile here,

Until the Son of God appear.

Chorus: Rejoice! Rejoice! O Israel!

To thee shall come Emmanuel.

O come Thou Rod of Jesse, free

Thine own from Satan's tyranny;

From depths of hell Thy people save,

And give them vict'ry o'er the grave. (Chorus.)

Veni, Veni, Emmanuel

Veni, veni Emmanuel! Captivum solve Israel

Qui gemit in exilio Privatus Dei Filio.

Chorus: Gaude, Gaude, Emmanuel! Nascetur pro te, Israel.

Veni, O Jesse Virgula! Ex hostis tuos ungula

De specu tuos tartari, Educ, et antro barathri. (Chorus.)

O Come, Divine Messiah

O come, Divine Messiah.

The world in silence waits the day

When hope shall sing its triumph

And sadness flee away.

Chorus: Sweet Saviour haste;

Come, come to earth;

Dispel the night and show thy face,

And bid us hail the dawn of grace. (Chorus.)

Shalt come in peace and meekness,

And lowly will thy cradle be;

All veiled in human weakness,

Thy majesty we'll see. (Chorus.)

O Come All Ye Faithful

O come all ye faithful, joyful and triumphant,

O come ye, O come ye to Bethlehem;

Come and behold Him, Born the King of Angels;

Chorus: O come, let us adore Him,

O come let us adore Him, O come let us adore Him,

Christ the Lord!

Sing choirs of Angels, Sing in exaltation,

Sing all ye citizens of Heav'n above:

Glory to God, in the highest glory. (Chorus.)

Adeste Fideles

Adeste fideles, Laeti triumphantes;

Venite, venite in Bethlehem;

Natum videte, Regem angelorum:

Chorus: Venite adoremus, Venite adoremus,

Venite adoremus Dominum.

Deum de Deo, Lumen de lumine,

Gestant Puellae viscera;

Deum verum, Genitum non factum. (Chorus.)

Angels We Have Heard On High

Angels we have heard on high,

Sweetly singing o'er the plains,

And the mountains in reply,

Echoing their joyous strains.

Chorus: Glo---ria, in excelsis Deo.

Glo---ria, in excelsis Deo.

Shepherds, why this jubilee?

Why your joyous strains prolong?

What the gladsome tidings be

Which inspire your heavenly song? (Chorus.)

Silent Night

Silent night! Holy night!
All is calm, all is bright.
Round yon Virgin Mother and Child!
Holy Infant, so tender and mild,
Sleep in heavenly peace!
Sleep in heavenly peace!

Silent night! Holy night!
Shepherds quake at the sight!
Glories stream from Heaven afar,
Heavenly hosts sing "Alleluia!"
Christ the Savior is born! Christ the Savior is born!

The First Noel

The first Noel the Angel did say.

Was to certain poor shepherds

In fields where they lay:

In fields where they lay keeping their sheep

On a cold winter's night that was so deep.

Chorus: Noel, Noel, Noel, Noel,

Born is the King of Israel.

They looked up and saw a star

Shining in the East beyond them far,

And to the earth it gave great light,

And so it continued both day and night. (Chorus.)

We Three Kings

We three Kings of Orient are,

Bearing gifts we traverse afar

Field and fountain, moor and mountain,

Following yonder star. (Chorus.)

Oh, star of wonder star of might,

Star with royal beauty bright,

Westward leading, still proceeding,

Guide us to the perfect Light.

O Sacred Head Surrounded

O Sacred Head, surrounded, By crown of piercing thorn!

O bleeding Head, so wounded, Reviled and put to scorn!

Death's pallid hue comes o'er Thee, The glow of life decays,

Yet angel hosts adore Thee And tremble as they gaze.

I see Thy strength and vigor All fading in the strife,

And death, with cruel rigor, Bereaving Thee of life;

O agony and dying! O love to sinners free!

Jesus, all grace supplying, O turn Thy face on me!

In this Thy bitter passion, Good Shepherd, think of me,

With Thy most sweet compassion, Unworthy though I be;

Beneath Thy Cross abiding, Forever would I rest,

In Thy dear love confiding, And with Thy presence blest.

At The Cross Her Station Keeping

At the cross her station keeping,

Stood the mournful Mother, weeping,

Close to Jesus to the last.

Through her heart, His sorrow sharing,

All His bitter anguish bearing,

Now at length the sword had passed.

O how sad and sore distress'd

Was that Mother highly blest

Of the sole-begotten One!

119

Ye Sons and Daughters of the Lord!

Alleluia! Alleluia! Alleluia!

Ye sons and daughters of the Lord!

The King of glory, King adored,

This day Himself from death restored. Alleluia!

Alleluia! Alleluia! Alleluia!

All in the early morning grey

Went holy women on their way

To see the tomb where Jesus lay. Alleluia!

Jesus Christ is Ris'n Today, Alleluia!

Jesus Christ is ris'n today, Alleluia!

Our triumphant holy day, Alleluia!

Who did once upon the Cross, Alleluia!

Suffer to redeem our loss, Alleluia!

Hymns of praise then let us sing, Alleluia!

Unto Christ our heav'nly King, Alleluia!

Who endured the Cross and grave, Alleluia!

Sinners to redeem and save. Alleluia!